Puzzle MANIA

BRAIN BENDERS

Puzzle Mania Brain Benders
First published in 2007 by Budget Books Pty Ltd
45–55 Fairchild Street,
Heatherton VIC 3202 Australia

© Budget Books Pty Ltd 2007

2 4 6 8 10 9 7 5 3
08 10 12 11 09

ISBN 978 1 7418 1436 1

Printed and bound in India

BEST FRIENDS

Write the names of the objects into the grid. Then rearrange the letters in the shaded squares to spell out the name of my best friend.

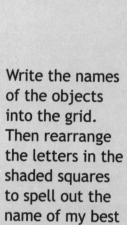

RAVING ROBOT

Cross out the letters that appear more than once and then rearrange the leftover letters to see what has happened to Robbie the Robot.

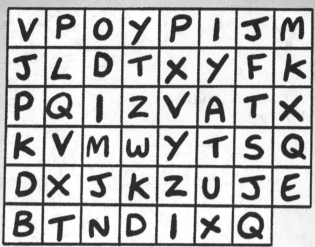

V	P	O	Y	P	I	J	M
J	L	D	T	X	Y	F	K
P	Q	I	Z	V	A	T	X
K	V	M	W	Y	T	S	Q
D	X	J	K	Z	U	J	E
B	T	N	D	I	X	Q	

2

WHICH WAY?

Can you help the Easter Bunny through the maze to reach his basket of eggs?

Hot Shot!

Which route should Sam take to reach his ball?

TRIANGULAR

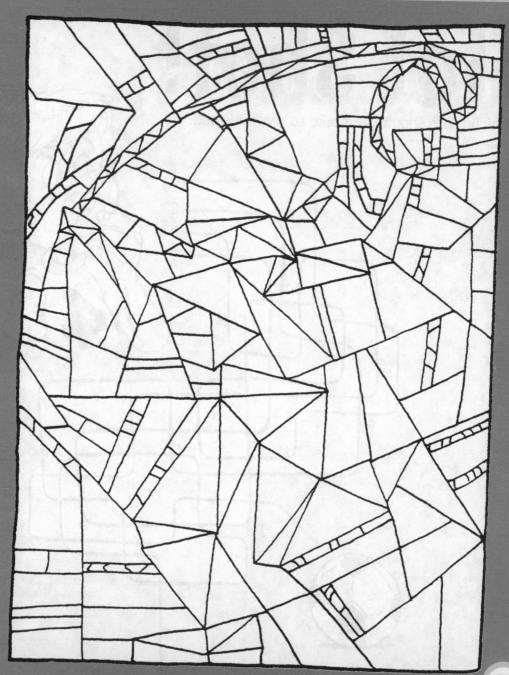

Fill in only the triangles and you will see a hidden picture.

BRICK BUILDER

How many bricks are missing from the wall?

FISH DISH

See if you can find the names of the fish below in the wordsearch!

SWORDFISH
TROUT
SQUID
OYSTER
SALMON
TUNA
SOLE
WHITEBAIT

```
Y O N E T D A Y M Y
E S W O R D F I S H
S A S O O L E S O T
T L P R U A W N L O
E M D N T S A S E D
R O W H T H A Q R E
D N I C N K Y U O M
W H I T E B A I T F
A M Y U E G G D C S
Y L T N A N D H I P
A L R A O Y S T E R
```

SKI FIT

Fit the skiing words into the grid.

3 LETTERS

FIT
ICE
SUN

4 LETTERS

FLAG
HARD
LONG
SKIS
SNOW
SOFT
STOP
THAW
TIME

5 LETTERS

BENDS
JUMPS
PISTE
POLES
SKILL
SLIDE
TREES
WEAVE

6 LETTERS

COURSE
FINISH
GLOVES
SKIING
SLALOM
SLOPES
SMOOTH

7 LETTERS

BALANCE
LANDING

8 LETTERS

CABLE CAR
DOWNHILL
MOUNTAIN
PRACTICE

9 LETTERS

CHAIRLIFT

10 LETTERS

INSTRUCTOR
SPECTATORS
SUNGLASSES

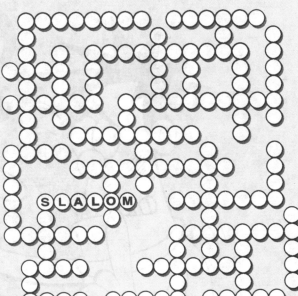

SLALOM

CRACKPOT

Oh, no!! I've broken my mom's vase. Which is the missing piece?

Dog Lead

Cross off all the letters in the grid that appear more than once and the leftover letters will spell out a breed of dog.

C	D	T	A	H	B
O	C	K	X	K	P
H	S	M	E	S	P
D	R	A	T	D	M

Snake Fake

Can you find four names of snakes?

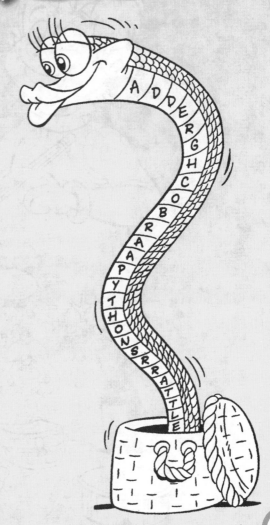

CLUED UP

Fill in the boxes below using the picture clues!

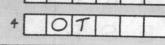

1 | |O|T| | |

2 | |O|T| | |

3 | |O|T| | | |

4 | |O|T| | |

5 | | |O|T| |

6 | |O|T| |

7 | |O|T| |

8 | | |O|T|

SUDOKU

Each row, column, and box must contain only one of each number from 1 to 9.

	2		8		9	6	7	
			1	5				
	8				4		1	2
		8						6
3	4			6			5	1
1						7		
8	1		4				9	
				9	3			
	6	5	7		1		2	

Worm Turn

Can you help this bird through the maze to reach the worm?

Dinosaur Double

Which two dinosaurs are the same?

Crossword

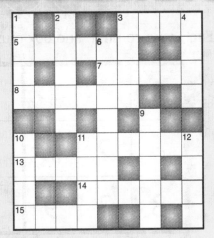

ACROSS

3. Stand idly about (4)
5. Program of business for a meeting (6)
7. Asian country (5)
8. Reach any place (6)
11. Land (6)
13. Souvenir (5)
14. Fabric with short, close pile (6)
15. Distance (4)

DOWN

1. Volcanic discharge (4)
2. Convey over water (5)
3. Country road (4)
4. Level (4)
6. Legal separation (7)
9. Arc (5)
10. Passenger vehicle (4)
11. Donate (4)
12. Fruit of the palm tree (4)

Sudoku

Each row, column, and box must contain only one of each number from 1 to 9.

5					7			
	2	7			5			9
8	3	9						
2		1		5			9	
	4		6		3		5	
	9			4		7		6
						3	1	5
4			5			9	7	
			2					4

Cross out the letters that appear more than once to reveal what I'll be when I leave school.

A	J	B	D	M	S	C
P	R	V	H	F	E	M	W
	W	S	B	N	V	C	J
	A	B	M	L	O	D	X
C	S	H	G	A	Y	J	R	E
G	X	I	D	F	C	W	E	Y
H	D	Q	X	V	K	N	Y	Q
R	Z	K	A	Z	T	Z	A	N

18

Vowel Veg

All the vowels are missing from this list of vegetables. Can you put them back?

1 SPRGS	6 TRNP
2 BRCCL	7 PTT
3 CBBG	8 CRRT
4 CLFLWR	9 PTT
5 LTTC	10 SPNCH

SPOT THE DIFFERENCE

Can you spot ten differences between the two pictures?

Join the Dots

Starting at no. 1, take your pencil and connect all the dots to make a secret picture.

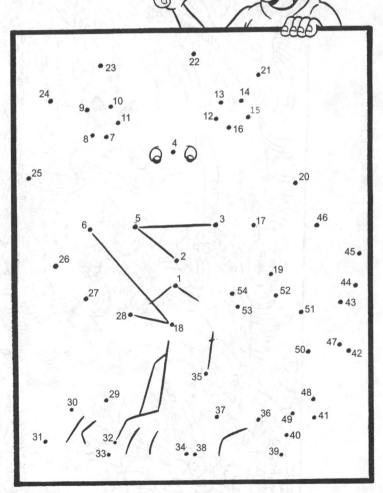

OUT FOXED

All the creatures in the forest hide when the fox is around!
Can you find six mice and four rabbits?

Chef's Piece

Can you spot which piece is from the picture?

Egg Timer

See if you can find the twelve words listed below in the wordsearch.
The words can go across, up, down, and diagonally!

YOLK

BOILED

BOX

CUP

SHELL

EGGS

FRIED

GOOSE

WHITE

HEN

POACHED

SCRAMBLED

SuDoKu

Each row, column, and box must contain only one of each number from 1 to 9.

	4		9		8	7	3	
8				1		6		9
2					6			4
							9	2
	8			3			5	
5		4						
7			2					3
1		2		6				7
	3	8	7		5		1	

25

BALLOONEY

Which two balloons out of this bunch are exactly the same size?

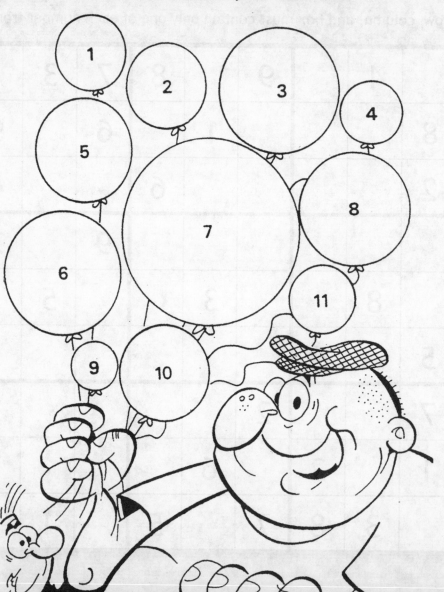

26

Name Frame

Find the letters hidden in the picture and rearrange them to spell out the girl's name.

APRIL SHOWERS

Storm clouds are gathering for some April showers!
How many clouds are there in the sky?

Carrot Cake

WHICH CARTOON IS THE ODD ONE OUT ?

BATHTIME

Look in the soapy bubble chain to find the names of seven things you would take into the bath with you.

Fishy

Can you find which fish is the odd one out?

Tool Bagged

TRIANGULAR

Fill in only the triangles and you will see a hidden picture.

Flower Potty

Which of the two silhouettes exactly matches that of the smiling sunflower?

Which flower face matches the original picture?

Film Fan

Rearrange the letters to spell out the titles of seven DVD films!

ON THE HOOK

Which line leads from the cat to the fish?

ON THE BUTTON

Which remote control button operates Lisa's CD player?

37

Chip List

Unscramble the letters in each packet of chips to find the five different flavors.

Waiter Go!

Hey kids, study this cartoon for 30 seconds, then cover it over and see if you can remember all the items on the waiter's tray!

Face Facts

Which face is the same as "A"?

BIRD BOX

Help our birdwatcher to identify the five birds he is watching. Place three boxes together to find the name of a bird.

BLA	WOO	NIG	CHA	PHE
DPEC	FFI	AS	CKB	HTING
IRD	ANT	KER	ALE	NCH

ROUTE RINGER

Can you help Phil through the maze to reach his cell phone?

BEEP! BEEP!

CROSSWORD

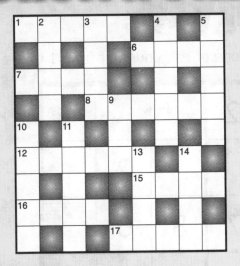

ACROSS
1. Women's garment (5)
6. Small stones (4)
7. Stalk (4)
8. Fine dust (6)
12. They bring rain (6)
15. One of an identical pair (4)
16. Number (4)
17. Fruit (5)

DOWN
2. Flown in a wind (4)
3. Slope (4)
4. Group of lions (5)
5. Bad weather (5)
9. Aged (3)
10. Cake topping (5)
11. Noise (5)
13. Halt (4)
14. Where corn is ground (4)

SPOT THE DIFFERENCE

Can you spot ten differences between the two pictures?

Sudoku

Each row, column, and box must contain only one of each number from 1 to 9.

6	7			5	2			
	8		4					2
					7		8	6
		3				1	4		6
		4		8			9	
8		2	9				5	
	2	7	3					
	1				8			5
			7	9			4	1

MAIL BOX

Using the grid references, work out where each of the eight squares is featured in the original picture.

PLANT FOOD

Which picture is the odd one out?

Link Up

Can you link up each of the words on the left with one of the words on the right to make eight longer words?

SHORE	OVER
CHAR	LINE
IS	ORE
THIN	MING
REST	MAN
NIGHT	LAND
DISC	KING
CHAIR	CLUB

48

Top Trauma

Arrghh! What a mess! Which splat is the same as the one on my top?

49

PICTURE PART

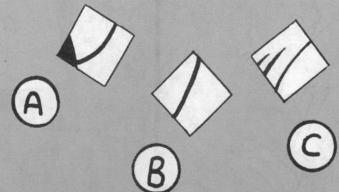

Which two squares are from the picture?

Just the Opposite

Can you help Laura unscramble the words to form a pair of opposites on each line?

1 SATF _ _ _ _ LWSO

2 DBA _ _ _ GDOO

3 NI _ _ _ UOT

4 RBEAK _ _ _ XIF

5 WLO _ _ _ _ GIHH

6 SATRT _ _ _ PTSO

7 IRNEWN _ _ _ _ SOLER

8 LAL _ _ _ _ NNEO

Spot the Difference

Can you spot the ten differences between the two pictures?

SHOPALOT

Find the clothing words in the grid.

```
L I K I G T M N P T S I G
S B D R E S S V T A T E H
N P E K L B X R S R I D W
A D C U L F A B I O G M U
E A B O Q I C K M F H R R
J M U S A U S U I T T R A
B S M U V T B N O R S Y E
E T C B Y I N N T O I X W
A P B L Z F A P S U J L R
N O C N X S E O H S K A E
T N U P H A U M P E L C D
S W V O A R F N O R S B N
N I G H T D R E S S P W U
```

BLOUSE
DRESS
SUIT
JACKET
SHOES
SKIRT
HAT
COAT
JEANS
TIGHTS
TROUSERS
UNDERWEAR
NIGHTDRESS

EVEN MORE SHOPS!

53

Sudoku

Each row, column, and box must contain only one of each number from 1 to 9.

4		6	9	5		8	7	
8		9	7					
				8	3	9		
	6							4
			1	6	7			
3							1	
		2	6	3				
					4	1		9
	1	4		9	5	7		2

Hard to Swallow

Which two pieces are not part of the picture?

Peter's Plan

Color in the shapes with a dot and rearrange the letters to reveal what exactly Peter has planned.

Monster Match

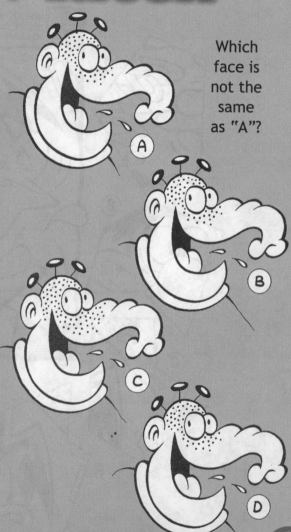

Which face is not the same as "A"?

A

B

C

D

Very Fishy

Which silhouette exactly matches the picture of the swordfish?

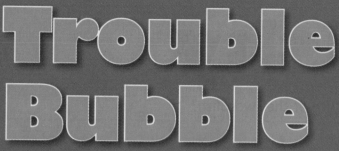

Trouble Bubble

Yee-ha!!
Can you find
these words in
the bubblechain?

WILD WEST

HORSE

COWBOY

TEXAS

SALOON

SHERIFF

59

Tear Full

This baby has just woken up and wants his bottle! How many tears is he crying?

Picture Pairs

Can you pair
the pictures?

Two at a Time

Draw some lines joining two circles together – A to A, B to B and so on. But remember, no two lines must cross!

DAY TO DAY

All these words are connected with DAY.

ANY	PAYDAY
BIRTHDAY	REST
ELECTION	SATURDAY
EVERY	SOME
FIRST	SUNDAY
FRIDAY	THURSDAY
HOLIDAY	TUESDAY
LAST	WEDDING
MODERN	WEDNESDAY
MONDAY	WEEKDAY
NEXT	WORKING
ONE	YESTERDAY

```
B L Y L E K Y A D Y A P C
Y N H A O L T A E J S R N
A K Y A D S E N D E W E Y
D F W E R H Y C U N X I W
N M R I S A T Q T T U E F
O I F I D T A R B I E S Y
M G N I D D E W I K O A D
N O L E J A O R D B D N S
C O D T V R Y A D S E U T
H I S E K E Y E R A O H T
G A U I R F R U N Z Y M S
L P N X O N H Y E O G T E
D G V S A T U R D A Y A R
```

Sudoku

Each row, column, and box must contain only one of each number from 1 to 9.

8		3		6	1			
7	4	5						1
	1		5			2		
				7		8	3	
		6		8		5		
	8	7		3				
		2			4		6	
3						9	1	5
			6	1		3		2

Ball Baffler

Can you help this boy through the maze to reach his ball?

In Sequence

Can you complete
the following sequences?

1. B F J N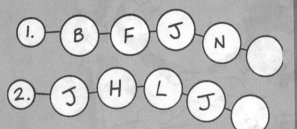

2. J H L J

66

Fish Face

Which
fish
is the
same
as "A"?

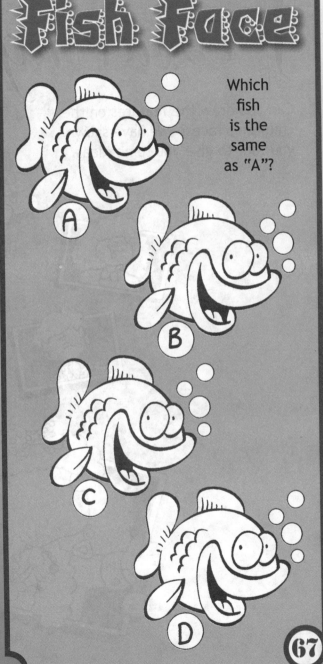

A

B

C

D

67

Featuring...

Can you draw the features on the children's faces? We have shown you four to give you some ideas.

Bubble Bands

Can you find the names of five pop favorites in the bubblechain?

Spot the Difference

Can you spot the ten differences between the two pictures?

HOWDY PARTNER

Answer these clues to reveal a hidden word (down from the arrow).

1. Name for a person that works with horses and cattle (6)

2. Law enforcement officer (7)

3. A place where cowboys relax (6)

4. A place with very little water or vegetation (6)

5. A criminal (6)

6. A cowboy's favorite food (5)

7. A cowboy rides this animal (5)

8. A state in the USA (5)

1. _ _ _ _ _ O
2. H _ _ _ _ _ _
3. _ _ L _ _ _
4. _ _ S _ _ T
5. O T A _ _ _
6. _ _ _ N S
7. _ R _ _ _
8. _ _ X _ _

Egg Head

Junior's favorite breakfast is a boiled egg with toast. Can you tell how many eggs he's dreaming about?

Edible Eight

Can you find the names of eight of my favorite food and drinks?

Eye Test

Susie has dropped her contact lenses and is trying to find them! Can you change "FIND" to "LENS" in three moves by changing one letter at a time?

Spot the Difference

Can you spot the ten differences between the two pictures?

75

76

To the Point

Which path should the arrow take to hit the apple?

Take Shape

Try to draw this angular diagram into the square by connecting some of the dots with your pencil. You must connect eight dots, but which ones?

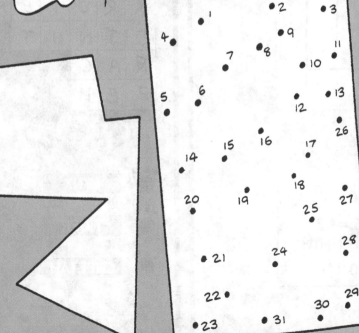

Spiral Sixes

Can you put the answers to the sums connected with six into the spiral? Start from the outside and put the answers in clockwise, all the way into the center. The last letter of one word is the first letter of the next, and so on...

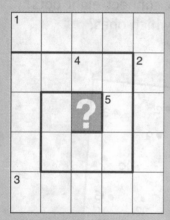

1. 72 ÷ 6

2. 3 x 6

3. 15 x 6

4. 7 x 6 = 42. Is this right?

5. 6 x 10

Cat Call

Find the seven types of cat in the grid. There's one other animal hiding in there too. Can you find it?

O	L	X	N	Y	L	L	T	P
T	I	G	E	R	E	O	I	H
B	O	A	E	O	C	R	A	G
E	N	O	P	E	E	T	E	R
A	D	A	L	H	E	L	I	O
R	R	O	T	E	N	A		
D	T	N	H	T				
R	A	C						
P	E	H						

 LYNX

 LEOPARD

 TIGER

 PANTHER

 CHEETAH

 LION

 OCELOT

TAIL TELLER

Which tail belongs to which mouse?

TRIANGULAR

Color in all the triangles to reveal a picture!

Man's Best Friends

1. T C A R I
   V I
   O

2. M D
   N A A
   A

3. O E
   E E G
   G R

4. A E
   N
   A R D

5. E D
   W
   N R
   A

Unscramble the letters to find the names of my five friends.

Rocket Route

Find your way through the rocket.

HAIR PIECE

Arrghh!!! Call that a haircut?
Can you find the missing piece?

A

B

C

Sudoku

Each row, column, and box must contain only one of each number from 1 to 9.

5		2		7			4	8
	8	9				7		
		1		2				3
	2	5			3			
			7		8			
			2			3	7	
6				3		5		
		7				1		3
2	3			1		8		9

Cook's Chaos

The cook has burnt the lunch again!
Can you find a way from the "A" to the frying pan?

87

Solve the math problem on the left and then find the
answer to the problem hidden in the number on the right.

$$50-16 = 262340$$

$$21+9 = 307151$$

$$82+11 = 659313$$

$$76-25 = 451542$$

$$48+43 = 703291$$

$$29-12 = 517643$$

$$67-31 = 983650$$

$$16+7 = 237427$$

$$33-18 = 764157$$

Tree Time

STARTING AT THE LETTER "C," MOVE FROM ONE SQUARE TO THE NEXT — TO FIND THE NAMES OF SIX TREES. USE EACH SQUARE ONLY ONCE

C	E	K	M	L
A	D	A	P	A
R	B	O	E	P
E	E	R	A	E
C	H	P	I	N

89

Sounds Like...

Beauty Route

Which path should this girl take to reach her lipstick?

Weather Report

Color in the shapes with a dot and rearrange the letters to reveal what the weather will be like today.

Magic Square

Can you put the words into the square, helped by the clues? The words read the same down as across.

1.			
2.			
3.			
4.			

1. Overtake
2. Against
3. Knock senseless
4. Perform a song

Rain or Shine

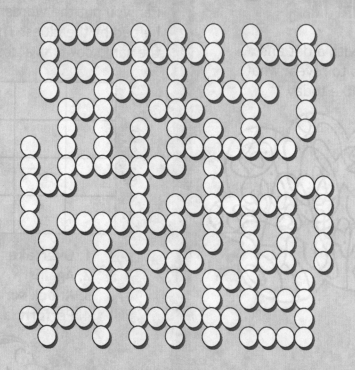

3 LETTERS

AIR
DRY
END
HOT
ICE
ICY
LOW
SUN

4 LETTERS

CALM
DULL
GUST
HEAT
MIST
RISE
ROAR
SNOW
VEER
WARM
WEST
WILD

5 LETTERS

CHILL
LEAST
SHINE
SLATY
UNFIT
WINDY

6 LETTERS

BRIGHT
HEAVEN
RANDOM
SQUALL
WINTER
ZEPHYR

7 LETTERS

BRACING
DRIZZLE

RAVAGED
STRATUS
SUNSPOT
TEMPEST
THERMAL
TORNADO

8 LETTERS

SPLUTTER
THUMPING

There are eight things in the bottom panel that are different from the top panel. Can you find them?

95

Sudoku

Each row, column, and box must contain only one of each number from 1 to 9.

	5	1					3	
9			1	3	8		4	
		6			7		1	
							9	7
		3	4		5	2		
2	8							
	9		5			4		
	4		2	1	3			8
	6					1	7	

Wild Thing

Write the answers to the clues and discover the mystery animal in the boxes below the arrow!

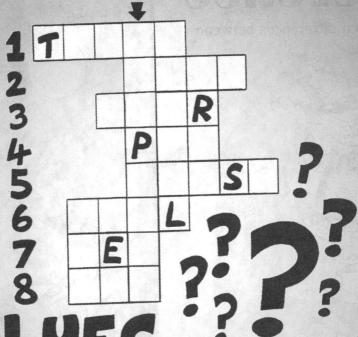

1 T
2
3   R
4 P
5   S
6 L
7 E
8

CLUES

1 Big cat
2 King of the jungle
3 Teddy or grizzly...
4 Farm animal
5 People ride this animal
6 This animal lives in water
7 Female chicken
8 A type of rodent

Spot the Difference

Can you spot ten differences between the two pictures?

Work It Out

Without using a pen to write your calculations down, can you work out the sum?

$$\bigcirc = -8 \quad \times 2 \quad +2 \quad -7 \quad \times 2 \quad +1 \quad \times 3 \quad 3$$

CAKE MIX

Can you change "CAKE" to "TYPE" in three moves?

Give Us a Clue

Find the words in the grid, then make an answer to the clue in the shaded squares.
Shaded clue: Country.

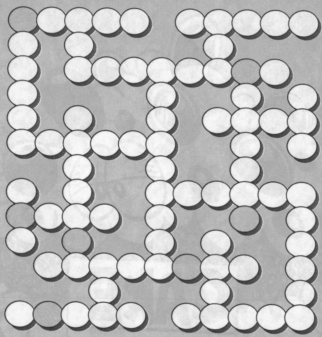

3 LETTERS		6 LETTERS	8 LETTERS
BUS	TREE	ALKALI	ADHESIVE
PEN	WARM	ICECAP	SPACIOUS
HUM	WEST	SUMMER	
TWO	WILD	TIGHTS	9 LETTERS
USE			
	5 LETTERS	7 LETTERS	COMPUTERS
4 LETTERS	AMBER		
	CLEAR	LEOPARD	
OVAL	PALMS	UPRIGHT	
SEAT	STORK		

Solutions

Puzzle 1

1	S	H	O	E
2	B	O	N	E
3	F	I	S	H
4	C	O	A	T
5	S	O	C	K
6	P	E	A	R
7	T	R	E	E
8	N	A	I	L

KATIE is the best friend's name.

Puzzle 2

		O			
	L				F
			A		
		W		S	
			U		E
B		N			

Puzzle 3

Puzzle 4
Route 3.

Puzzle 5

Puzzle 6
25 bricks.

Puzzle 7

Y	O	N	E	T	D	A	Y	M	Y
E	S	W	O	R	D	F	I	S	H
S	A	S	O	O	L	E	S	O	T
T	L	P	R	U	A	W	N	L	O
E	M	D	N	T	S	A	S	E	D
R	O	W	H	T	H	A	Q	R	E
D	N	I	C	N	K	Y	U	O	M
W	H	I	T	E	B	A	I	T	F
A	M	Y	U	E	G	G	D	C	S
Y	L	T	N	A	N	D	H	I	P
A	L	R	A	O	Y	S	T	E	R

Puzzle 8

C	A	B	L	E	C	A	R		F	I	N	I	S	H	
H					S					C			C	O	
A		W		S	U	N	G	L	A	S	S	E	S		O
T	I	M	E		K			I		O		M			U
R		A		I			D	F		O		O			R
G	L	O	V	E	S		S	P	E	C	T	A	T	O	R	S
I		E				U					T		H		E
F			D	O	W	N	H	I	L	L		H			
S	T	O	P			A			M				L		
L				I	N	S	T	R	U	C	T	O	R		O
O					N	D			U				N		
P		S	L	A	L	O	M		L	A	N	D	I	N	G
E		K				W			T						B
S	K	I	I	N	G			P	R	A	C	T	I	C	E
		L							O			I		R	N
	F	L	A	G			B	A	L	A	N	C	E		D	S
	I								E			E		E	S
T	H	A	W		J	U	M	P	S		P	I	S	T	E

Puzzle 9
Piece B.

Puzzle 10
Boxer.

Puzzle 11
The four snakes are Adder, Cobra, Python, Rattle.

Puzzle 12
1. Potato, 2. Root,
3. Mother, 4. Bottle,
5. Tooth, 6. Pot,
7. Moth, 8. Cot.

Puzzle 13

4	2	1	8	3	9	6	7	5
6	3	7	1	5	2	9	8	4
5	8	9	6	7	4	3	1	2
7	9	8	3	1	5	2	4	6
3	4	2	9	6	7	8	5	1
1	5	6	2	4	8	7	3	9
8	1	3	4	2	6	5	9	7
2	7	4	5	9	3	1	6	8
9	6	5	7	8	1	4	2	3

Puzzle 14

Solutions

Puzzle 15
A and B.

Puzzle 16
Across: 3. Loaf,
5. Agenda, 7. India,
8. Arrive, 11. Ground,
13. Relic,14. Velvet,
15. Mile.

Down: 1. Lava,
2. Ferry, 3. Lane,
4. Flat, 6. Divorce,
9. Curve,10. Tram,
11. Give, 12. Date.

Puzzle 17

5	1	4	9	2	7	6	3	8
6	2	7	3	8	5	1	4	9
8	3	9	4	1	6	5	2	7
2	6	1	7	5	8	4	9	3
7	4	8	6	9	3	2	5	1
3	9	5	1	4	2	7	8	6
9	7	2	8	6	4	3	1	5
4	8	6	5	3	1	9	7	2
1	5	3	2	7	9	8	6	4

Puzzle 18
Pilot.

Puzzle 19
1. Asparagus,
2. Broccoli,
3. Cabbage,
4. Cauliflower,
5. Lettuce,
6. Turnip,

7. Pea, 8. Carrot,
9. Potato, 10. Spinach.

Puzzle 20

Puzzle 21

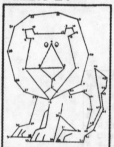

Puzzle 22

Puzzle 23
Piece C.

Puzzle 24

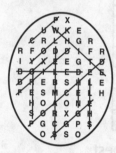

Puzzle 25

6	4	1	9	2	8	7	3	5
8	5	3	4	1	7	6	2	9
2	7	9	3	5	6	1	8	4
3	1	6	5	8	4	9	7	2
9	8	7	6	3	2	4	5	1
5	2	4	1	7	9	3	6	8
7	6	5	2	4	1	8	9	3
1	9	2	8	6	3	5	4	7
4	3	8	7	9	5	2	1	6

Puzzle 26
3 and 6 are
the same.

Puzzle 27
Amanda.

Puzzle 28
15 clouds.

Puzzle 29
Cartoon C.

Solutions

Puzzle 30

Puzzle 31
No. 4

Puzzle 32
Screwdriver No. 5.

Puzzle 33

Puzzle 34
1 and A.

Puzzle 35
1. *Gladiator*, 2. *Tarzan*,
3. *The Beach*, 4. *Rugrats
the Movie*, 5. *Jaws*, 6. *The
Iron Giant*, 7. *Mulan*.

Puzzle 36
Line 3.

Puzzle 37
Button 1.

Puzzle 38
1. Ranch, 2. Sour cream,
3. Plain, 4. Cheese,
5. Vinegar.

Puzzle 40
Face B.

Puzzle 41
Blackbird, Woodpecker,
Nightingale, Chaffinch,
Pheasant.

Puzzle 42

Puzzle 43
Across: 1. Skirt,
6. Grit, 7. Stem,
8. Powder, 12. Clouds,
15. Twin, 16. Nine,
17. Apple.

Down: 2. Kite,
3. Ramp, 4. Pride,
5. Storm, 9. Old,
10. Icing, 11. Sound,
13. Stop, 14. Mill.

Puzzle 44

Puzzle 45

6	7	9	8	5	2	1	3	4
3	8	1	4	6	9	7	2	5
2	4	5	1	3	7	8	6	9
7	9	3	5	2	1	4	8	6
1	5	4	6	8	3	9	7	2
8	6	2	9	7	4	5	1	3
4	2	7	3	1	5	6	9	8
9	1	6	2	4	8	3	5	7
5	3	8	7	9	6	2	4	1

Solutions

Puzzle 46
1. C3, 2. D2, 3. A1, 4. B2, 5. E1, 6. B4, 7. F4, 8. D3.

Puzzle 47
Picture 3. (Hole on wristwatch strap)

Puzzle 48
Shoreline, Charming, Island, Thinking, Restore, Nightclub, Discover, Chairman.

Puzzle 49
Splat C.

Puzzle 50
Squares B and C.

Puzzle 51
fast-slow, bad-good, in-out, break-fix, low-high, start-stop, winner-loser, all-none.

Puzzle 52

Puzzle 53

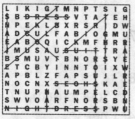

Puzzle 54

4	3	6	9	5	2	8	7	1
8	5	9	7	1	6	2	4	3
2	7	1	4	8	3	9	5	6
1	6	7	3	2	8	5	9	4
9	4	5	1	6	7	3	2	8
3	2	8	5	4	9	6	1	7
7	9	2	6	3	1	4	8	5
5	8	3	2	7	4	1	6	9
6	1	4	8	9	5	7	3	2

Puzzle 55
Pieces C and E.

Puzzle 56
Date.

Puzzle 57
Face C.

Puzzle 58
Silhouette A.

Puzzle 59

Puzzle 60
48 tears.

Puzzle 61
1. King - 11. Queen,
2. Snakes - 13. Ladders,
4. Bat - 16. Ball,
5. Bread - 12. Cheese,
6. Bucket - 3. Spade,
7. Skull - 15. Crossbones,
9. Cat - 8. Mouse,
14. Fish - 10. Chips.

Solutions

Puzzle 62

Puzzle 63

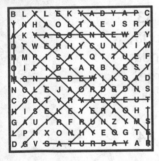

Puzzle 64

8	2	3	7	6	1	4	5	9
7	4	5	2	9	3	6	8	1
6	1	9	5	4	8	2	7	3
2	5	1	9	7	6	8	3	4
4	3	6	1	8	2	5	9	7
9	8	7	4	3	5	1	2	6
1	9	2	3	5	4	7	6	8
3	6	4	8	2	7	9	1	5
5	7	8	6	1	9	3	4	2

Puzzle 65

Puzzle 66

1. B (+4 letters),
F (+4 letters),
J (+4 letters),
N (+4 letters) = R.

2. J (−2 letters),
H (+4 letters),
L (−2 letters),
J (+4 letters) = N.

Puzzle 67

Fish D.

Puzzle 69

Puzzle 70

Puzzle 71

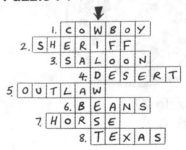

Solutions

Puzzle 72
Eight.

Puzzle 73
19 boiled eggs.

Puzzle 74
1. Chocolate,
2. Pizza,
3. Chicken,
4. Burgers,
5. Ice cream,
6. Curry,
7. Coffee,
8. Steak.

Puzzle 75
Find, Fend,
Lend, Lens.

Puzzle 76

Puzzle 77
Path D.

Puzzle 78

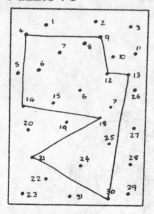

Puzzle 79
1. Twelve,
2. Eighteen,
3. Ninety,
4. Yes, 5. S

Puzzle 80

L	X	N	Y	L	L		
T	I	G	E	R	E	O	H
B	O			O	C	R	A
E	N		P	E	E	T	
A		A	L	H	E		
R	R	O	T	E			
D	T	N	H				
A	C						
P							

Puzzle 81
1-B, 2-A, 3-C.

Puzzle 82

Puzzle 83
1. Victoria,
2. Amanda,
3. George,
4. Andrea,
5. Andrew.

Puzzle 84

Solutions

Puzzle 85
Piece A.

Puzzle 86

5	6	2	3	7	1	9	4	8
3	8	9	4	5	6	7	1	2
4	7	1	8	2	9	6	5	3
7	2	5	1	9	3	4	8	6
1	4	3	7	6	8	2	9	5
8	9	6	2	4	5	3	7	1
6	1	8	9	3	4	5	2	7
9	5	7	6	8	2	1	3	4
2	3	4	5	1	7	8	6	9

Puzzle 87

Puzzle 88

50-16	=	262340
21+9	=	307151
82+11	=	659313
76-25	=	451542
48+43	=	703291
29-12	=	517643
67-31	=	983650
16+7	=	237427
33-18	=	764157

Puzzle 89

Puzzle 90
1. I, 2. C, 3.P, 4.J, 5.Q,
6.T, 7.B, 8.U, 9.Y, 10.O.

Puzzle 91
Path D.

Puzzle 92

Puzzle 93
1. Pass, 2. Anti,
3. Stun, 4. Sing.

Puzzle 94

(crossword grid with words: WILD, WARM, ROAR, AIR, SUN, ICE, CALM, SHINE, SQUALL, GUST, HEAVEN, SUNFIT, WEST, STRATUS, TEMPEST, TORNADO, DRIZZLE, DRY, HOT, LOW, RISE, END)

Puzzle 95

(spot-the-difference image)

Puzzle 96

8	5	1	6	2	4	7	3	9
9	2	7	1	3	8	5	4	6
4	3	6	9	5	7	8	1	2
5	1	4	3	8	2	6	9	7
6	7	3	4	9	5	2	8	1
2	8	9	7	6	1	3	5	4
1	9	8	5	7	6	4	2	3
7	4	5	2	1	3	9	6	8
3	6	2	8	4	9	1	7	5

Solutions

Puzzle 97
1. Tiger, 2. Lion,
3. Bear, 4. Pig,
5. Horse, 6. Seal,
7. Hen, 8. Rat.

Mystery animal:
ELEPHANT.

Puzzle 98

Puzzle 99
The answer is 22.

Puzzle 100
Cake, Take, Tape, Type.

Puzzle 101

A	M	B	E	R		S	T	O	R	K
L		U				W				
K		S	P	A	C	I	O	U	S	
A				O		P		P		P
L		L		M		T	R	E	E	
I	C	E	C	A	P			I		N
		O		U		U		G		
U		P		T	I	G	H	T	S	
S	E	A	T		E			T		U
E		R		E	R	O				M
	A	D	H	E	S	I	V	E		M
		U				A				E
P	A	L	M	S		C	L	E	A	R

Country: Austria.